Music

Alan Blackwood

Titles in this series

Art
Cinema
Communications
Farming
Fashion
Industry
Medicine
Music
Science
Sport
Transport
Warfare

Editor: Tracey Smith
Designer: Ross George

Front cover *The Happy End are a young British big band. Their repertoire ranges from the work of such composers as Kurt Weill and Charles Ives to Cuban Rhumbas, Township Jazz and the music of the innovative jazz musician Thelonious Monk. The Happy End, with its energetic and enthusiastic performance style, is representative of the many groups to have found popularity by creating a fusion of popular and classical styles of music.*

Frontispiece *Annie Lennox and Dave Stewart, lead singer and guitarist for one of the most successful Scottish pop groups of the 1980s.*

Back cover *Louis Armstrong is one of the best-known personalities in the world of jazz. From the early 1920s he worked with such musicians as Joe 'King' Oliver and Fletcher Henderson and produced much innovative playing and singing for his own well-known bands.*

First published in 1989 by
Wayland (Publishers) Ltd
61 Western Road, Hove
East Sussex BN3 1JD, England

British Library Cataloguing in Publication Data
Blackwood, Alan, 1932–
Music. – (The Twentieth century).
1. Music, 1900–
I. Title II. Series
780'.904

ISBN 1–85210–626–3

Typeset by L. George & R. Gibbs, Wayland
Printed by G. Canale and C.S.p.A., Turin, Italy
Bound by Casterman, S.A, Belgium

Contents

Sounding a New Note

At the end of the nineteenth century, much 'serious' music was written on a large scale: orchestras and choirs were often huge and symphonies and operas long. Music tended to be grand and majestic. Wagner had done the most to develop music in this way, and at the beginning of the new century, some composers were happy to follow in his footsteps. Others had new ideas.

Below left *Claude Debussy, shown here when a young man.*

Below right *Both Maurice Ravel (pictured here) and Claude Debussy were fine pianists.*

Mammoths and Impressionists

Gustav Mahler and Richard Strauss were the best known of the composers who carried on the Wagnerian style. Mahler wrote nine huge symphonies, including *The Symphony of a Thousand*, so called because it needs so many musicians and singers to perform it. Strauss composed massive symphonic poems, such as *An Alpine Symphony*. In this piece, also written for a colossal orchestra, there is the musical description of a vivid sunrise over the mountains, a scramble across a dangerous glacier and a frightening thunderstorm.

Other composers, though, rebelled against such sensational music. The Frenchmen Claude Debussy and Maurice Ravel were two such musicians. People often call these composers 'musical impressionists', because in some of their music they aimed to convey the same kind of images, moods and feelings as the Impressionist painters. To achieve this artistic effect in music, they used subtle but daring new harmonies and rhythms.

Debussy's most famous orchestral piece is *La mer*. He wrote it for a large orchestra, but for much of the time he used the instruments quite sparingly, to evoke the sea in all its moods. He also wrote such marvellously evocative piano pieces as *Claire de lune* (Moonlight), *Jardins sous la pluie* (Gardens in the Rain), and *Poissons d'or* (Goldfish). As well as impressionistic music, Ravel wrote pieces like *Bolero*, which is a clever parody of a dance.

It was Debussy and Ravel, rather than Mahler and Strauss, who pointed the way forward for much twentieth-century music. Strauss and Mahler, however, adapted and extended many of the musical forms that had been developed by earlier composers. Their use of chromatic harmony and their inventive handling of the orchestra became characteristic of their compositions for both voices and instruments.

It was an innovative approach to musical texture and harmony that led to musicians such as Debussy being described as the first of the modern composers.

Above Debussy was strongly attracted to oriental art. This print of a giant sea wave by the Japanese artist Hokusai is said to have helped to inspire the composition of his orchestral piece La mer.

New out of old

Another way in which composers at the beginning of this century turned away from Wagner, and struck out in new directions, was through the use of folk music such as traditional songs and dances. Earlier composers, notably Liszt and Brahms, had sometimes made arrangements of folk songs and dances, but many critics have said that they had made them sound pretty and respectable, and had destroyed their true character.

In Britain, Ralph Vaughan Williams studied his country's folk music, and made effective arrangements of such lovely old melodies as *Greensleeves*. In Hungary, Béla Bartók took folk music more seriously still. He travelled around his own country, and up into the hills and mountains of neighbouring Transylvania (legendary home of Count Dracula), taking note of hundreds of age-old folk songs and dances. These fascinated him, because the rhythms, scales and harmonies

Right *Much of Béla Bartók's music is fiery and passionate, but the composer was a shy, quiet man.*

Below *A scene from* The Firebird *(1910). This was the first of three ballet scores written by Stravinsky for the Russian impresario Sergei Diaghilev. The music and the choreography of these works were both controversial and innovative.*

Left Igor Stravinsky, one of the most influential composers of the twentieth century, shown here soon after he arrived in Paris from the USSR. He lived in France and Switzerland before finally taking American citizenship and settling in California in 1945.

they used were so new and exciting to his ear. Bartók then recreated many of their melodies, harmonies and rhythms in his own compositions. To some listeners, such compositions as his piano piece *Allegro barbaro* sounded wild and discordant. To others, they were excitingly different.

Igor Stravinsky did not research folk music as Bartók had done, but he loved the old songs and dances of his Russian homeland. He became famous when he wrote the music for three ballets, *The Firebird*, *Petrushka* and *The Rite of Spring*. Stravinsky wrote brilliantly for a large orchestra. At the same time, his harmonies and rhythms also sounded new and strange, because of his use of Russian folk song and dance. Indeed, the barbaric sound of his music for *The Rite of Spring* (a ballet about pagan religious rites in ancient Russia) so shocked the audience at the first performance in Paris, in 1913, that there was a riot. Stravinsky went on composing for another fifty years, but never created another sensation like it.

Above *An exciting ballet production of Schoenberg's song-cycle* Pierrot lunaire. *This picture captures well the 'dream-like' quality of the music.*

A new freedom

In Vienna, Arnold Schoenberg began his career by writing music that sounded as rich and heavy as that of Mahler and Strauss. But he broke away from this style when he wrote some of the first atonal music.

For a long time music had been written 'in a key'. For example, a piece could be described as being written 'in G major', which usually meant that the music began and ended with the chord of G major. All the harmonies and melodies in the piece could be labelled in terms of the key of G major. This was tonal harmony. Other composers since Wagner had been moving away from writing music in this way, but it was Schoenberg who made the break with musical conventions and abandoned tonal harmony altogether.

Schoenberg used atonal music very effectively in such pieces as *Erwartung,* in which a singer tells of how she wanders through a wood at night and finds the body of her murdered lover. Such music has been described as Expressionist, and has been compared to the work of a group of painters, of the same period and collective name, who were concerned with the expression of inner feelings, as opposed to external impressions.

Another such work was Schoenberg's *Pierrot lunaire* (Moonstruck Pierrot), which uses a vocalist and five instrumentalists to convey a strange, dream-like, sometimes nightmarish mood. For this piece, Schoenberg developed a new way of using the voice, called, in German, *Sprechgesang*, which is halfway between singing and speaking. His pupil, Alban Berg, used a form of *Sprechgesang* in his opera *Wozzeck*, which is about a poor, mentally persecuted soldier.

Schoenberg and Berg were living in Vienna at the same time as Sigmund Freud, the Austrian psychoanalyst and pioneer of modern psychology. There is a close connection between such music as *Pierrot lunaire* and *Wozzeck* and Freud's theories about dreams and the subconscious workings of our minds.

Left *Alban Berg was a strikingly handsome man. Unlike his close friends Schoenberg and Webern, Berg lived quite comfortably.*

Below *A scene from Berg's opera* Wozzeck. *Here the miserable soldier Wozzeck is being laughed and shouted at. Later in the opera he is driven to murder.*

A new order

Schoenberg, and his pupils Berg and Anton Webern, continued to write atonal music, but Schoenberg was not entirely happy with the new freedom which it gave them. Somehow, writing music with no rules at all was much more difficult than working within the old rules of tonality!

In the early 1920s Schoenberg devised a new way of writing music, known as twelve-note or serial composition. These terms describe a piece of music based on twelve different notes ordered in a way

Right *Anton Webern was ignored by most musicians, attacked by Hitler's Nazi government, and accidentally killed by an American soldier at the end of the Second World War. Today he is recognized as one of the century's most influential composers.*

peculiar to that piece; music was composed using these notes instead of the usual eight notes of the major or minor scales used in tonal music. All the chords and melodies in a serial piece can be explained in terms of a series, an ordering of the twelve chosen notes.

Schoenberg's ideas were not entirely new. Other composers, including Debussy, had also thought of different musical scales. But Schoenberg worked out his twelve-note system very thoroughly, to create music that sounded totally new and strange. It produced an effect that was quite like hearing a foreign language for the first time. Audiences were puzzled and perplexed, but his ideas have since been used by many other composers during this century.

Berg and Webern were quick to take up this new way of composing, and each developed it in his own way. Berg proved that serial music could still be full of emotion, particularly with his *Lyric Suite* for string quartet, inspired by a love affair, and his Violin Concerto, written in 1935, just before his death.

Webern, wrote extremely short, concentrated pieces, which were expressive, but in a very restrained way.

The percussion section
The most remarkable section of a big orchestra is the percussion. This section includes the kettledrums, side and bass drums, an array of gongs and cymbals, the xylophone and the closely related glockenspiel, tubular bells, the triangle, the celesta (a kind of miniature piano with a tinkling sound), and also such special-effects instruments as the wind machine, which, with a revolving drum inside a casing of canvas or other fabric, makes a sound like rushing wind.

Technically speaking, such instruments as the wind machine are not percussion instruments, since nothing is actually struck in their performance. They are, however, regarded as members of the percussion family. Richard Strauss in his Alpine Symphony *and Ravel in his ballet music for* Daphnis and Chloë *have written parts for this instrument.*

Above *Arnold Schoenberg was a great teacher as well as a composer. He is shown here lecturing at an American university, after he had settled in the USA.*

Left *The celesta, one of the more unusual instruments included in the percussion section of a large orchestra.*

Above Vesta Tilley (left) and Marie Lloyd (right), two stars of the London music halls. These portraits are taken from sheet music covers for two of their songs.

Songs of peace and war

While Debussy, Bartók and Schoenberg were pioneering new sounds and ideas, people went on singing and whistling the kind of songs they loved. They heard many of these in the music hall and vaudeville theatres of the time.

The stars of the music hall were nearly all singers. Most of them, in fact, did not have very good singing voices. What mattered was their stage personality, and getting hold of a good song. The big stars of the London music halls, such as Marie Lloyd, Vesta Tilley and George Robey, regarded their songs as their personal property, singing them over and over again, often in several different theatres each night.

Music hall songs like 'A Little of What You Fancy Does You Good' were very funny, but it is interesting how many expressed the plight of the poor people of those days, while still managing to sound bright and cheerful. 'Two Lovely Black Eyes' turns the spotlight on street or family violence. 'My Old Man Said Follow the Van' is about a poor family that has to flee from its home at night, because it cannot pay the rent. But the tunes of these songs make you think everyone is having a wonderful time!

Songs like these were still being written during the First World War. British troops marched off to the horrors of the front-line trenches singing 'Pack Up Your Troubles in Your Old Kit Bag' and 'It's a Long Way to Tipperary'. There were patriotic songs too. Edward Elgar, probably the greatest British composer of the time, had written the *Enigma Variations* for orchestra and other beautiful works. But it was the words of 'Land of Hope and Glory', actually written by somebody else to a melody from one of his marches, that made him a national hero during the war.

Above *An artist's impression of soldiers leaving a London station to return to the Western Front during the First World War.*

Left *Edward Elgar, pictured in 1904. By the time of the First World War he had composed his greatest symphonies, concertos and oratorios. It was, however, his patriotic war-time song 'Land of Hope and Glory' that brought him popular acclaim.*

13

All that Jazz

At the beginning of the First World War (1914-18), jazz was still just the local music of New Orleans in the south of the USA. By 1930 it was a popular musical style throughout the Western world.

Jazz comes to town

The first jazz musicians were far too poor to go to a school or music academy. They taught themselves, and because hardly any of them could read music, they improvised, that is, made up the music as they went along. They earned money playing in funeral processions, or in New Orleans' many bars, cafés and brothels.

There were some very talented people among these musicians, who soon made a name for themselves. Joe 'King' Oliver and his 'Creole Jazz Band', the pianist

Below Joe 'King' Oliver's jazz band in 1922, also featuring the young Louis Armstrong (centre) on trumpet. The line-up of early jazz bands was largely modelled on the old military bands of the American Civil War (1861-5).

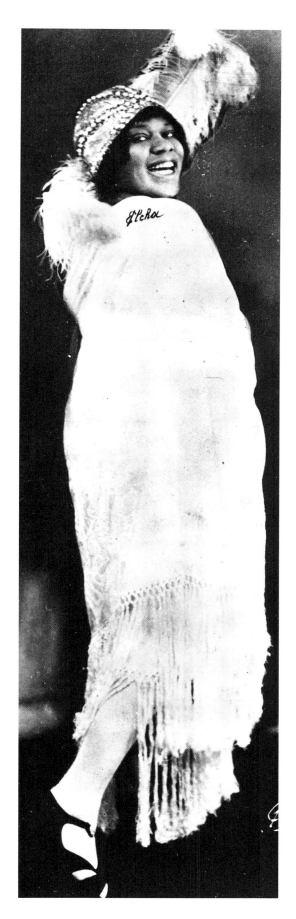

Ferdinand 'Jelly Roll' Morton and his band of 'Red Hot Peppers', and the trumpeter Louis Armstrong, were three pioneering instrumentalists. There were great singers, too; Ma Rainey and Bessie Smith were women with strong voices, used to singing in crowded, noisy saloons, or in the open air.

During and after the First World War, black musicians moved up the Mississippi river to cities further north, especially to St Louis, Chicago and New York. In this way jazz spread across America. There was an exciting new form called boogie-woogie, which was like a speeded-up blues. And white musicians, such as cornet player Leon 'Bix' Beiderbecke, began to play jazz.

This was the age of Prohibition (1920-33), when the United States government banned the sale of alcoholic drinks, and such notorious gangsters as Al Capone organized the illicit liquor trade. Many jazz musicians played in nightclubs called Speak easies, run by gangsters. As a result of the use of such venues, early jazz was associated with people and places outside respectable society.

Left Bessie Smith was one of the first and greatest jazz vocalists. She did more than any other performer to elevate the blues into a socially acceptable art form.

Below Alberta Hunter was an important blues singer. She performed with many well-known musicians, including Fletcher Henderson, Louis Armstrong and Fats Waller. In 1922 she composed Downhearted Blues, which was recorded the following year by Bessie Smith, who made it famous.

Right Thomas Alva Edison, seen here testing an early model of his phonograph. He is listening to the sounds through a kind of stethoscope.

Far right A shot from the film 'Round Midnight, *which is about a saxophone player living in Paris. The role of the saxophonist is played by the jazz musician Dexter Gordon.*

Jazz on the air

A lot of people in Europe and the USA may have called jazz brash and noisy and even thought of it as sinful music. But it still spread like wildfire. This was thanks largely to the gramophone and the radio.

Back in 1877 the American inventors Thomas Alva Edison and Alexander Graham Bell had made the first experimental sound recordings. By the early years of this century, making and selling records was already a widespread and profitable business.

Below Two children listening to a large gramophone in 1934.

The saxophone
A prominent instrument of the big dance bands was the saxophone. This interesting cross between a woodwind and brass instrument was invented in the nineteenth century by a Belgian instrument maker, Adolphe Sax. He intended it to be used in military bands, but it really became popular this century with the rise of jazz and dance music. No doubt Monsieur Sax would have been astonished to see the gleaming saxophone section in a dance band, usually ranging in size and tone from the small, high soprano to the large, deep baritone saxophone. Some of the finest jazz musicians have been saxophonists, including Lester Young, Charlie Parker, Ben Webster, Coleman Hawkins, Stan Getz and John Coltrane. Debussy, Ravel, Darius Milhaud and Vaughan Williams are some of the many composers of this century who have written music for the saxophone.

The first commercial recordings were described as acoustic. Sounds were recorded directly on to a phonograph cylinder or gramophone disc. Performers had to sit or stand as close as possible to a large 'horn' that received the sounds and transmitted them on to wax. When opera stars such as Enrico Caruso and Nellie Melba made recordings, there was only room for a small orchestra as well. It was easier to record a small band, which is why early recordings made by such jazz pioneers as Jelly Roll Morton and Bessie Smith sounded so good and were so successful. When electric recording was invented in the 1920s, whole operas and symphonies could be recorded satisfactorily, but jazz and dance music were still the most popular records.

The Italian inventor Guglielmo Marconi, meanwhile, had developed radio transmission and reception to a high enough standard for public broadcasting. In the 1920s radio broadcasting joined the gramophone in the business of spreading music, especially the new dance music, around the world. Soon many homes in the USA and Europe had a radio set as well as a gramophone. Following the American Wall Street stock market crash of 1929, and the world-wide economic Depression, dance music over the radio helped to cheer everybody up. If people had lost their jobs and had very little money, music may have helped them to forget their own problems.

__Below__ A recording session of about the year 1900. It is easy to see the acoustic horns used in the early recording processes.

Jazz everywhere

The energetic beat of jazz, and its distinctive harmonies, found their way into almost every other kind of music. They galvanized the songwriters of Tin Pan Alley, New York's old music publishing district. Instead of the sentimental ballads, which people had loved to sing in their homes round the parlour piano, Irving Berlin wrote songs like 'Alexander's Ragtime Band'.

The new dances, first on record and then heard over the radio, had lively, syncopated, jazzy rhythms and some odd, catchy names: Cakewalk, Foxtrot, Black Bottom, and best known of all, the Charleston, named after a town in the

American state of South Carolina. There was also a craze for Latin-American dances (from Central and South America), which were quite similar to the syncopated rhythms of jazz. Most popular and fashionable of these was the Tango.

Everybody was caught up in this exciting new musical scene. Debussy wrote his piano piece *Golliwog's Cakewalk* for his little daughter 'Chou Chou', and Ravel wrote a piece actually called *Blues*. In the German capital city of Berlin, the composer Kurt Weill wrote music for satirical operas full of jazzy rhythms and harmonies, including the song known in English as 'Mac the Knife'. Back in America, George Gershwin, who also started as a songwriter in Tin Pan Alley, wrote a jazz piano concerto, the famous *Rhapsody in Blue*. A few years later he composed a whole opera, *Porgy and Bess*, about black people in the 'Deep South' of the United States, where jazz had started.

Even Stravinsky, the great Russian composer of *The Rite of Spring*, loved jazz. After he moved to the United States, he wrote his *Ebony Concerto* in 1945, especially for the jazz clarinet player and dance-band leader Woody Herman.

Above left *The American song writer Irving Berlin.*

Above *This illustration shows couples dancing the tango, one of many popular dances based on Latin-American rhythms. The stylized forms used in this drawing are designed to express the exaggerated movements of the dance.*

Left *A scene from a production during the late 1980s of George Gershwin's jazz-inspired opera* Porgy and Bess.

Swinging It

Out of all the bright and jazzy songs and dances of the early days of radio came the mainstream of popular music of the 1930s - the music of swing.

The Big Band sound

Paul Whiteman was an American band leader who claimed he had 'made a lady out of jazz'. He wrote out arrangements of songs and dances for his band, instead of allowing the players to improvise, and he included violins, which made the band sound more like an orchestra. In short, he gave the rhythms and harmonies of jazz a smooth and shiny gloss. This was not so much a case of turning jazz into a lady as giving it the musical equivalent of the haircream that was so popular with men at the time!

Swing may sometimes have sounded smooth and glossy; but that did not mean it was dull. The big American swing bands were led by men of great talent and flair: Woody Herman, Benny Goodman and Artie Shaw were brilliant clarinet players; Tommy Dorsey and Glenn Miller were equally proficient on the trombone. These were all white musicians. 'Count' Basie and 'Duke' Ellington were black musicians, whose bands kept closer to the strong, bouncy rhythms of true jazz. Ellington, in fact, not only arranged the

Below left *The flamboyant American band leader Paul Whiteman. Such brilliant musicians as Leon 'Bix' Beiderbecke played in his band.*

Below right *Duke Ellington, one of the greatest figures in jazz. He was an eminent composer as well as a band leader.*

Above *Frank Sinatra (left) and Bing Crosby (right) pictured early in their highly successful careers as singers and actors.*

Right *Singer Billie Holliday performing with the celebrated American vibraphone player Lionel Hampton.*

music for his band, but composed such popular classics as *Mood Indigo, Caravan* and *Sophisticated Lady*.

A feature of the big swing bands of the USA and Europe was their use of vocalists. They came in with the early days of broadcasting, and at first they sang fairly softly, to avoid damaging the large but delicate microphones. The equipment was soon improved, but vocalists carried on singing in a soft, intimate and sentimental way which was very different from the style of the old stars of music hall or early jazz. This was crooning. Bing Crosby and Frank Sinatra, two superstars of showbusiness in years to come, began their careers as crooners. Billie Holliday was a singer who combined crooning with jazz to beautiful effect.

The Great White Way

The bouncy steps of the Charleston and the jaunty tunes and rhythms of ragtime and swing were soon seen and heard in the musical theatre, and especially on Broadway. This famous and glamorous street was New York's theatreland, called 'The Great White Way' because of its glittering lights. This was the home of the American musical, which grew out of the old traditions of Viennese operetta.

Tin Pan Alley's top songwriters all contributed to the huge success of the Broadway musicals. George Gershwin wrote the music to such great shows of the 1920s and 1930s as *Lady Be Good* and *Strike Up the Band*. Composer Richard Rodgers first teamed up with lyricist Lorenz Hart, to create, among other Broadway hits, *On Your Toes* and *Babes in Arms*. When Hart died, Rodgers formed an even more famous partnership with

Oscar Hammerstein, going on to produce *Oklahoma*, *Carousel* and *South Pacific*. Irving Berlin's greatest Broadway hit was *Annie Get Your Gun*, inspired by the true story of Annie Oakley, a sharpshooter who joined a famous travelling circus.

The stories and scenarios of the great Broadway musicals were often as cleverly written as the music. Another brilliantly gifted American song writer, Cole Porter, mixed Shakespeare's comedy *The Taming of the Shrew* with a modern storyline in *Kiss Me Kate*. *Guys and Dolls*, with music by Frank Loesser, was based on short stories by Damon Runyon, a writer who knew all about the real life crooks and other colourful characters who once lived on and around Broadway. *My Fair Lady*, by Alan Lerner and Frederick Loewe, set to music the story of George Bernard Shaw's witty social comedy *Pygmalion*, which tells of a London flower-seller who becomes a society lady to win somebody else a bet.

Below *Marlon Brando as Sky Masterson, singing 'Luck be a Lady Tonight' in the film version of the musical* Guys and Dolls.

Broadway goes to Hollywood

Below *Judy Garland as Dorothy with her three friends, the tin man, the scarecrow and the cowardly lion in the film* The Wizard of Oz.

When singing star Al Jolson, in the film *The Jazz Singer*, declared, 'You ain't heard nothing yet folks!', he really meant it. The year was 1927, and with those famous words, he ushered in the era of 'talking' films or movies.

In fact, the invention of the film soundtrack meant that the audience heard just as much music as 'talk', as *The Jazz Singer* had already made clear. The impresarios of Broadway (the businessmen who invested in the big stage musicals) soon realized there were even bigger profits to be made by putting musicals on to the screen. So, many of the great Broadway song writers, and many of the stars of the Broadway stage, went to Hollywood, home of the American cinema industry.

Above Shirley Temple at the height of her fame.

Above left Perhaps the most celebrated scene in the history of the screen musical: Gene Kelly singing the title song from Singin' in the Rain.

Successful stage musicals were adapted for the cinema. Cameras could move close in, or swing high above the studio sets, creating visual effects impossible on any theatre stage. This inspired a new style of musical, even more spectacular than the Broadway shows. The new-style Hollywood musicals created their own superstars as well.

Fred Astaire was already a Broadway dancer when he arrived in Hollywood to sing and dance his way to international fame in *Top Hat*, *Easter Parade* and many more musicals conceived specially for the cinema and for him. A few years later, Gene Kelly, another superb dancer, crowned his film career with *An American in Paris* and *Singin' in the Rain*. There was also little Shirley Temple, who became the world's number one box-office attraction, aged seven, singing 'On the Good Ship Lollipop' and 'Animal Crackers in my Soup'. Then Judy Garland shot to stardom when she stepped in for Shirley Temple in the enchanting fairy-tale musical *The Wizard of Oz*.

The film industries of Britain, Germany, France and Italy all made musicals too. But none could rival Hollywood.

Above Gone with the Wind *was not a musical, but it inspired some of the best-known film music. Its stars were Clark Gable and Vivien Leigh.*

More movie music

There was plenty of music in the movies, once sound recording had been developed. Indeed, in the 1930s many films had virtually continuous music from start to finish. There were types, or styles, of music for everything - a ship at sea, a stage coach being chased by bandits, a beautiful sunset. There was one kind of music to make you feel romantic, and

another kind to make you feel scared. Much of it was only intended as background sound, while the actors and actresses spoke their lines.

Providing such film music was like writing to a kind of musical formula, and most of it sounded much the same. It was, nevertheless, a specialized and expert craft, since the duration of the music had to be calculated with the accuracy of a stop-watch, to match each film sequence.

Some composers made it a real art. Erich Korngold was an opera composer in Vienna before he moved to Hollywood, and set new standards in the quality of movie music. Another Austrian-born composer, Max Steiner, also went to Hollywood where he wrote the score to perhaps the most celebrated film ever made, *Gone with the Wind*.

Other eminent composers wrote music for films, as composers of earlier times had provided incidental music to stage plays. The American Aaron Copland was awarded a Hollywood Oscar for some of his scores, while the British composer Arthur Bliss wrote some stirring music to the early science-fiction film *Things to Come*. Far away from Hollywood, the Soviet film director Sergei Eisenstein commissioned Sergei Prokofiev to write music for his historical dramas *Alexander Nevsky* and *Ivan the Terrible*. Prokofiev's vivid and exciting music helped to make these films classics of the cinema.

Below *A scene from the Soviet film* Alexander Nevsky, *showing the battle between the Russians and the invading Teutonic Knights. Prokofiev wrote its exciting score.*

Right Dmitri Shostakovich survived many political crises, particularly during Joseph Stalin's years of power. He has been acclaimed as one of this century's greatest composers.

Below The tyrannical rule of Adolf Hitler caused immense misery to many musicians and composers. Hitler held strong views on the quality of new music, literature and art and the styles which were acceptable within his society. He is shown here listening to German folk music during a picnic.

Music and politics

The music of the movies and the swing dance-bands provided marvellous 'escapist' entertainment for millions of people in Europe and the USA during the years of the economic Depression. But elsewhere, musicians themselves could not escape from the politics of the times.

In Italy, the composer Luigi Dallapiccola, who conveyed liberal political views in some of his music, and the great conductor Arturo Toscanini, both spoke out against the dictatorship of Benito Mussolini and his Fascist government.

Then in 1933 Adolf Hitler and his Nazi Party came to power in Germany. Hitler hated Jews, and forced such German-speaking Jewish composers as Weill and Schoenberg into exile. It was not just Jewish artists who suffered. There was a ban on the music of Webern and another important German composer, Paul Hindemith, because Hitler objected to it.

When Joseph Stalin came to power in the Soviet Union, he insisted that composers had as much of a duty to serve the community as a factory worker. He accused Sergei Prokofiev and Dmitri Shostakovich of writing noisy and discordant music, and threatened to punish them if they did not write music that was instantly enjoyable. Stalin certainly was a terrible dictator and tyrant, but we

have his regime to thank for the delightful music Prokofiev then wrote for *Peter and the Wolf*, the thrilling score to his ballet *Romeo and Juliet*, and the infectious 'Snow Ride' from his music for the film *Lieutenant Kijé*.

In fact, even in countries where composers were free to work as they liked, some of them felt that much contemporary 'serious' music was too difficult for most people to enjoy, and that they should write in a more attractive style. Copland in the USA produced such tuneful ballets as *Billy the Kid* (about a notorious Wild-West outlaw), *Rodeo* and *Appalachian Spring*, and Benjamin Britten in Britain wrote his popular *Young Person's Guide to the Orchestra* for a documentary film, and *Let's Make an Opera!*, which invites the audience to join in the performance.

Left The Soviet composer Sergei Prokofiev.

Below The British composer Benjamin Britten, photographed near the Snape Maltings concert hall in Aldeburgh, Suffolk. This venue has become closely associated with both the performance of Britten's music and the training of young musicians at international masterclasses which are held there.

Back to War

There were only twenty-one years of peace between the end of the First World War in 1918 and the start of the Second World War in 1939. But the new wartime mood was quite different and music expressed this clearly.

Music's war effort

In 1939 British soldiers marched off to battle cheerily singing 'We're Going to Hang Out the Washing on the Siegfried Line' (referring cheekily to the main German line of defence) and 'Roll Out the Barrel'. But a year later the British and French armies had been defeated, and Britain faced invasion and the Blitz. The front line was now much nearer to home. It was now 'The People's War'.

In air-raid shelters and in London's tube stations deep beneath the streets, there were concert parties to take people's minds off the bombing. There were radio programmes such as 'Workers' Playtime', with music broadcast

Right London's underground stations became night-time shelters during the Blitz of the Second World War. Spontaneous and organized music-making in such shelters helped to keep people cheerful.

Left *Vera Lynn was Britain's most popular wartime singer. She is pictured here wearing the uniform of ENSA, the organization that provided entertainment for the armed forces.*

over factory loudspeakers to keep up the workers' morale. Most significant of all was the mood of many popular wartime songs. Vera Lynn (the 'Forces' Sweetheart') sang 'We'll Meet Again' and 'There'll be Blue Birds Over the White Cliffs of Dover', which were not at all jolly or patriotic, but simply expressed a strong hope for peace. 'Lili Marlene' was a German wartime song, which was just as wistful in mood.

The musical scene changed when the USA joined the Allies. American soldiers and airmen were not worn down by three years of air raids, black-out and rationing. They were fresh and eager to win the war. 'The Boogie-Woogie Bugle Boy from Company B' was the lively kind of song they liked. There was also Major Glenn Miller and his Army Airforce Band, who played such great numbers as 'In the Mood'. Few British people had heard swing music of that exciting quality before. They learnt to jive and jitterbug as well; such energetic dancing was a sign of things to come.

Salutes and memorials

Singers and dance bands were not the only musicians to bring music to the war effort. Composers were commissioned to write film music to stir the hearts of the people. William Walton, a leading British composer of symphonies, concertos and the choral work *Belshazzar's Feast*, proved how good he was at writing film music with his score for *The First of the Few*, about the man who designed the Spitfire fighter aircraft of Battle of Britain fame.

He was then asked by Laurence Olivier to write the music for a film of Shakespeare's *Henry V*, which was intended to raise British hopes of victory. Richard Addinsell was not as eminent a composer as Walton, but his *Warsaw Concerto* written for the film *Dangerous Moonlight*, about a Polish fighter pilot, made him famous. Though not intended for a film, Shostakovich's *Leningrad Symphony*, written while that city was being defended by the Red Army against the invading Germans, struck the same patriotic note.

Right *Laurence Olivier in the title role of the film of Shakespeare's* Henry V. *William Walton's music helped to make this a great morale-booster during the war.*

The experiences of war also inspired some of the most deeply felt music of our century. Shostakovich himself, like many creative and sensitive people, hated war, and he wrote several symphonies that expressed his horror of it. Back in Britain, Michael Tippett composed the oratorio *A Child of our Time,* which deals with the Nazi persecution of the Jews. It was movingly performed in Germany when the war was over. For the consecration of the new Coventry cathedral (built in place of the one that had been bombed), Britten wrote his *War Requiem,* which was written in remembrance of the death and destruction of both world wars. Schoenberg, who had been persecuted as a Jew, composed another oratorio-like piece, *A Survivor from Warsaw,* which described the plight of Polish Jews under the Nazis.

Above *A rather glamorized view of the Blitz. Anton Walbrook plays the 'Warsaw Concerto' in the film* Dangerous Moonlight.

Left *The reality of the war. This photograph shows the ruins of London's ancient Guildhall, after an air raid in 1940.*

Music Goes Electric

The world of popular music began to divide after the Second World War. Jazz musicians, notably saxophonist Charlie Parker and trumpeter Dizzie Gillespie, created a style called Bebop. Rock-and-roll, meanwhile, was turning the true world of popular music upside down.

Rock around the clock

The basic form and style of rock-and-roll (named after the kind of dancing that accompanied it) grew out of the old blues and boogie jazz styles, but possessed a vital new energy and drive. Bill Haley and his Comets first recorded 'Shake, Rattle and Roll', then, in 1956, 'Rock Around the Clock', for the film, *The Blackboard Jungle*.

This was the piece that really launched rock-and-roll, and caused riots in cinemas and dance halls when it was played. Chuck Berry caused almost as great a sensation, singing numbers like 'Roll Over Beethoven', and making audiences laugh and cheer with what he called his 'duck waddle' around the stage.

But the greatest sensation of all was Elvis Presley. His Mississippi childhood in the south of the USA gave him a feel for the rhythms of jazz, and when he wiggled his hips ('Elvis the Pelvis') and dropped his voice to a deep throb in hits like 'Hound Dog' and 'Jailhouse Rock', girls had hysterics. Anything to do with Elvis – records, films, clothes, jewellery – was a multi-million dollar business.

Right Chuck Berry, one of the first and finest stars of rock-and-roll, pictured here with his electric guitar.

34

Just as important as the new songs were the instrumental backings. The symbol of rock-and-roll was the guitar; not the classical or Spanish guitar, but a shiny plastic instrument, wired up to loud speakers, that produced a strong and strident sound. Electric guitars and drums were the instruments of rock-and-roll. To a new generation, the big dance bands seemed like musical dinosaurs, and very soon most of them were just as extinct.

Above *An impressive example of the electric organs which were installed in many cinemas of the 1920s and 1930s.*

The new hardware

For the millions of rock-and-roll fans of the 1950s, the electric guitar was their introduction to electrically aided or electronic music. But long before the Second World War, inventors and musicians had been interested in the connection between sound waves and electrical energy, and what could be done while changing the one into the other.

Pianos and violins were wired up so that the vibrations of their strings were converted into electrical impulses, which were then amplified and changed back into sounds. These were conventional instruments, which were simply modified by electrical means.

The theremin and the ondes martenot, both named after their inventors, were far more original. They used valves called oscillators to create electrical impulses

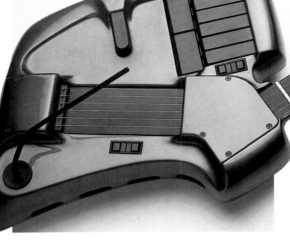

which were then converted into audible sound. The Hammond organ (also named after its inventor) worked on the same principle. Its great attraction was that it didn't need all the wind pipes of a conventional organ, and therefore took up only a fraction of the space. Modern variants of the electric organ or piano take up less space still.

Just after the Second World War came the invention of the tape recorder, which opened the way for the blending or mixing of recorded sounds. Finally, the American inventor Robert Moog created the ultimate electronic sound wonder, the synthesizer. The word 'synthesize' means to 'build up' or 'reconstruct', and this is exactly the function of a synthesizer. Oscillators create basic electrical sound-wave patterns, which can then be modified and combined, much as the colours of the spectrum might be blended into marvellous new shades and intensities of light. Add a 'sequencer', or computer, which can apply programmes involving millions of electrical signals, and a synthesizer opens up a whole new technological universe of sound.

Left *The SynthAxe, an instrument which is based on the design of an electric guitar, but operates more like a synthesizer.*

Below *A modern synthesizer.*

Above A scene from Stockhausen's opera Donnerstag aus Licht (Thursday from Light). This opera is the first in a cycle of seven operas which is to be written by Stockhausen during the late 1980s and early 1990s.

Electronic revolution

Many of the composers mentioned in this book so far continued to write music for large orchestras, or for such standard instruments as the piano, just as their predecessors had done. Others, however, believed that the music of our time, like building and design, should make use of advances in science and technology.

Olivier Messiaen in France has used the strange, other-worldly tones of the Ondes Martenot to add a new dimension to the exotic sound of his compositions. Edgard Varèse included factory and police sirens in some of his pieces. The American John Cage, a provocative thinker as well as composer, conceived one piece using twelve radio sets tuned to different frequencies. The music depended on whatever sounds came out of them. Cage thus pioneered the idea of aleatory music, that is, music which depends on the element of chance.

Just after the Second World War, composers of a new generation – Frenchman Pierre Boulez, Italian Luciano Berio and German Karlheinz Stockhausen – joined together in experiments with tape recorders. They recorded everyday sounds, such as people talking and railway trains, re-recorded them at slower or faster speeds, and cut up the tapes and reassembled them, until the original sounds came out as something entirely different. They called this *musique concrète* (concrete music) because it used sounds which existed around them, and because they actually 'built' the music in a physical way out of magnetic recording tape. Abstract artists had done something similar, when they took fragments of newspapers, clothing or other everyday items and stuck them together to create a totally new visual image, called a collage.

Boulez, Stockhausen and others have also combined traditional instruments or voices with aleatory and electronic systems in their music. Stockhausen's work called *Stimmung* (meaning 'atmosphere' or 'mood'), electronically mixes the individual voices of a small group of singers, to achieve a kind of hypnotic chant. Because the mixing depends on the spontaneous actions of an operator at the controls, each performance emerges as a new and unique experience. Such music has become very popular.

Below This photograph was taken during rehearsals for Donnerstag aus Licht. Stockhausen controlled the different electronic sounds and musical effects used in this opera from an electronic control panel. Stockhausen is one of today's most original and exciting figures in the realm of electronic music.

Anything Goes

By the 1960s there was 'light music' and there was 'pop'. In the past, styles of music had often been associated with social class, almost as much as dress or manner of speech. Pop music was different. It belonged to a certain age group, rather than a social class. It was the cult of the young, and it expressed a whole new way of life.

Pop goes bang

The first pop idols, Bill Haley and Elvis Presley, had been American, and their rock-and-roll was still quite close to jazz. The Beatles were British, and not as influenced by the heritage of jazz. Their huge success heralded the true age of rock, with its explosion of forms, styles and personalities. People talked of jazz rock, soft rock, soul rock, though the styles and the stars were changing all the time. Some styles, though, carried all before them.

There was hard rock or heavy metal, thundered out in discotheques to flashing lights and laser beams. The Rolling Stones, The Who, Led Zeppelin and other groups voiced the real rebellion of the young. Punk rock, deliberately crude and offensive, was an even stronger challenge to conventional law and order.

Below *The members of The Beatles, Ringo Starr, Paul McCartney, John Lennon and George Harrison. In the 1960s they created new fashions in clothes and hairstyles as well as in music.*

A type of rock called acid rock represented a retreat from the tough real world. 'Acid' was LSD, an hallucinatory drug, and acid rock groups echoed this in music. They gave themselves surreal or 'psychedelic' names. Such groups as Pink Floyd and Tangerine Dream used the technology of synthesizers to create weird or trance-like sounds, sometimes coming quite close to the music of such composers as Messiaen and Stockhausen.

Reggae was another colourful part of the rock scene. The reggae music of Bob Marley and the Wailers was connected with the Rastafarian religious cult. Its mixture of rock and Latin-American rhythms was taken up and enjoyed by a whole generation of young people, in both the USA and Europe.

Above *Pink Floyd in concert during the 1970s. This band uses visual effects as an important part of its performance. Their complex musical style often approaches the compositions of classical composers.*

Left *Bob Marley, the star of reggae music, died tragically at the age of thirty-five.*

Middle of the road

Rock and pop is the music of the young. But there are also millions of mums and dads, uncles and aunts, and they often prefer what the music business calls 'middle of the road'.

Types or categories of music that were once a part of the pop scene, such as 'rhythm and blues', 'soul' and 'country and western', have all shifted towards the middle of the road. Such singers as Bob Dylan, Joan Baez and Johnny Cash have played a part in this movement. Back in the 1960s such musicians had a big following among the young, especially in the USA, where they spoke out, or sang out, in favour of civil rights for blacks and against the Vietnam War. But the fairly traditional style of their songs has brought them a much wider popularity. Burt Bacharach, by comparison, stands much closer to the old traditions of Tin

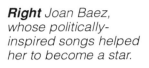

Right *Joan Baez, whose politically-inspired songs helped her to become a star.*

Below *Robert Redford, Katherine Ross and Paul Newman in* Butch Cassidy and the Sundance Kid. *The huge popularity of this film owed much to Burt Bacharach's song* Raindrops Keep Fallin' on my Head.

Pan Alley. His songs are wonderfully tuneful, while catchily up to date. He wrote the melody for the song 'Raindrops Keep Fallin' on my Head', which did much to make *Butch Cassidy and the Sundance Kid* such a successful film, though the song really has nothing to do with the story!

Stage and screen musicals are just as popular as ever, despite the loss of so many theatres and cinemas due to the growth of television. One of the first of the new-style musicals was *West Side Story*, with a thrillingly dynamic score by the composer and conductor Leonard Bernstein, who aims to combine quality with popularity in all his music. Stephen Sond-

heim wrote the lyrics to *West Side Story*, and has since become a top composer of sophisticated musicals. Andrew Lloyd Webber and Tim Rice caused much concern in show business when they started work on *Jesus Christ Superstar*. Mixing religion and entertainment seemed a risky thing to do. But the score, giving some of the rhythms and harmonies of rock a deeper meaning, has made it one of the great landmarks of musical theatre. They have collaborated on many highly successful musicals since then. Working both alone and in partnership, they are among the best-known figures in twentieth-century musical theatre, with box-office hits on both sides of the Atlantic.

Above A scene from the film version of West Side Story, *a brilliant stage and screen musical. This piece has been described as a modern-day* Romeo and Juliet *and owes much of its immense popularity to Leonard Bernstein's score.*

More new sounds

We have talked about 'serious', 'light' and 'pop' music, 'rock' and 'middle of the road'. There are dozens more labels which we can use to slot music into pigeon-holes. But during this century, many composers and musicians have attempted to give us a wider experience of the whole world of sound and music. Debussy loved the sound of the Javanese gamelan bands he heard in Paris, working their sounds into his compositions.

Bartók brought age-old folk music back to life while Ravel, Stravinsky, Copland, Walton and a host of other composers joined hands with jazz and dance music. Messiaen loves the sounds of oriental percussion and bird song,

translating these into a fascinating musical language of his own.

Today's composers are constantly creating other novel sound effects, which cut right across old-fashioned notions of 'classical', 'pop' or any other category of music. Composers such as Krzysztof Penderecki from Poland, and Hungarian-born György Ligeti have created amazing new concert pieces and operas, using micro-tonality (a tuning system requiring instruments or singers to sound notes which are extremely close in pitch). They have often asked singers to do such unusual things as whisper, hiss, whistle, or speak words very rapidly. The British composer Harrison Birtwhistle had the clever idea of turning a Punch and Judy show into an opera, conveying its crazy

Women composers

Until this century, women had little opportunity to be composers. The situation is different today. At the same time as women in Britain and America were campaigning for the right to vote, Ethel Smyth made a name for herself with dramatic operas such as The Wreckers, *which is about shipwrecks on the Cornish coast. In Britain, Elisabeth Lutyens, Elizabeth Maconchy, Thea Musgrave and Judith Weir, amongst others, followed her, with important operas and other compositions, using twelve-note techniques and other contemporary methods and styles. In America, such composers as Ruth Crawford-Seeger and Amy Marcy Beach have become highly respected for their many compositions.*

Left A Night At The Chinese Opera *by the British composer Judith Weir, which was first produced to great acclaim in the late 1980s.*

Left *This picture shows a scene from Philip Glass' opera* The Making of the Representative for Planet 8. *Glass is one of the best-known of the minimalist composers.*

violence with imaginative instrumental and vocal effects.

Minimalism is another new style of music that does not fit any of the old stereotypes. The term refers to the composer's ability to make a little (a minimal amount) go a long way, and the style has won new audiences for a group of American composers. Minimalists take snatches of melody and rhythm and play them again and again, changing a note or a beat at a time, so that the whole pattern of the music changes very gradually, like the colours and shapes of a kaleidoscope. Terry Riley, Steve Reich and Philip Glass use electronic and pre-recorded sounds, synthesizers and aleatory methods, as they weave their sometimes dazzling, sometimes soothing and hypnotic, tapestries of sound.

Glossary

Aleatory music   Music which uses chance in its performance or composition; from the Latin word *alea*, meaning 'dice'.

Atonal   Music that is written without any established key or tonality.

Bebop   Jazz style, often fast and frenetic, weaving notes round a melody.

Blues   Basic popular form, of twelve bars, using a special sequence of chords.

Boogie-woogie   Early jazz style, reminiscent of a speeded-up blues (*see above*).

Chromatic   The scale comprising the twelve semitones that make up an octave.

Chromatic harmony   Term used to describe music that frequently uses notes other than those of the major or minor key in which it is written.

Concerto   Composition for one or more solo instruments and orchestra.

Folk music   Music that develops among a specific race or community, and is usually not written down.

Harmony   Sounding together of two or more notes of different pitch.

Latin-American music   Mainly dance styles, originating in the Caribbean or South America, with characteristic rhythms, similar to jazz.

Opera   Stage drama or comedy set to music; operetta (little opera) is lighter and more tuneful in style.

Oratorio   Large concert work, usually for orchestra, chorus and vocal soloists, setting some religious or other serious text to music.

Pitch   'Highness' or 'lowness' of a musical note, measured by the frequency of its sound waves.

Ragtime   Early American style of popular music.

Rock   General name for many types of pop music.

Rock-and-roll   Early style of pop music, derived mainly from jazz blues and boogie.

Scale   Sequence of notes in ascending or descending order of pitch, the most common being the major or minor scales.

Serial music   Music which is composed by using the twelve notes of the chromatic scale in a fixed order chosen by the composer. This pattern of notes is known as the series.

Sprechgesang   German word (speech-singing) for vocal style, halfway between speaking and singing.

Swing   Popular music style, derived from jazz.

Symphonic poem   Orchestral composition describing scenes or events in music without words, often inspired by a story or poem.

Symphony   Large-scale orchestral composition, usually composed in four movements.

Syncopation   Rhythm which in some way disturbs the regularity of the basic beat of the music, by means of emphasis, displacing or slurring the beat.

Twelve-note music   A compositional technique closely related to serialism.

Vaudeville   A light theatrical entertainment containing musical and comedy acts.

Further Reading

Ardley, Neil **Music: An Illustrated Encyclopedia** (Hamlyn, 1986).

Bailey, Eva **Music and Musicians** (Batsford, 1983).

Blackwood, Alan **The Arts: Music** (Wayland, 1988).

Blackwood, Alan **Twenty Names in Classical Music** (Wayland, 1987).

Hayward, Philip **The Media: The Pop Music Business** (Wayland, 1988).

Hurd, Michael **The Oxford Junior Companion to Music** (OUP, 1979).

Kobal, John **A History of Movie Musicals** (Hamlyn, 1983).

Langley, Andrew **Twenty Names in Pop Music** (Wayland, 1987).

Lerner, Alan Jay **The Musical Theatre** (Collins, 1986).

Picture acknowledgements

The publishers would like to thank the following for allowing their illustrations to be reproduced in this book: Aldus Archive 40; Clive Barda 9 (bottom), 37 (bottom); The Bridgeman Art Library 5; Camera Press 42 (top); Donald Cooper (Photostage) 38, 45 (bottom left); Glyndebourne Festival Opera 19 (bottom); The Happy End (Jon Ingledew) *front cover;* Hulton Picture Library 11 (top), 14, 15 (both), 21 (bottom); Camilla Jessel 6 (bottom), 11 (bottom); Kent Opera 45 (top); The Kobal Collection 21 (top right and left), 24, 25 (right), 26, 27, 32, 33 (top); Mander and Mitchenson Theatre Collection 12 (both); Mary Evans Picture Library 4 (both), 6 (top), 7, 9 (top), 13 (both), 16 (top), 17 (bottom), 18, 19 (top right); Photri International 22 (top), 25 (left), 35 (top); Redferns *back cover;* Rex Features *frontispiece,* 45 (bottom); Ronald Grant 42 (bottom), 43; Topham Picture Library 8, 10, 16 (bottom), 17 (top), 19 (top left), 20 (both), 22 (bottom), 23, 28 (top and bottom), 29 (top and bottom), 30, 31, 33 (bottom), 34, 35 (bottom), 36, 37 (top), 39, 41 (both); Zefa 44.

Index